eco GUIDES

A Teen Guide to

Eco-Gardening, Food, and Cooking

Jen Green

Heinemann
LIBRARY
Chicago, Illinois

Edited by Andrew Farrow, Adam Miller, and
  Vaarunika Dharmapala
Designed by Richard Parker
Original illustrations © Capstone Global Library
  Ltd 2013
Illustrated by HL Studios
Picture research by Tracy Cummins
Originated by Capstone Global Library Ltd
Printed and bound in China by CTPS

16 15 14 13 12
10 9 8 7 6 5 4 3 2 1

Library of Congress Cataloging-in-Publication Data
Green, Jen.
A teen guide to eco-gardening, food, and cooking / Jen
Green.
p. cm.—(Eco guides)
Includes bibliographical references and index.
ISBN 978-1-4329-7046-8 (hb)—ISBN 978-1-4329-7051-2
(pb)
1. Teenagers and the environment. 2. Sustainable
agriculture. 3. Food habits. I. Title.

GE195.G715 2013
641.01—dc23

2012009955

Acknowledgments
We would like to thank the following for permission to
reproduce photographs: Alamy p. 39; Capstone Library
pp. 15, 17 (Karon Dubke); Corbis pp. 4 (© Antony
Nagelmann), 5 (© Daniela Buoncristiani/cultura), 8 (©
Ambient Images Inc.); Getty Images pp. 27 (Yellow Dog
Productions), 31 (Tetra Images), 37 (ML Harris), 46 (Tim
Bradley); Shutterstock pp. 11 (David Hughes), 13 (Perov
Stanislav), 19 (Pavel Mikoska), 20 (Claus Mikosch), 21
(tepic), 23 (chris2766), 26 (aleks.k), 28 (Frontpage), 29
(Dmitriy Shironosov), 30 (Richard Thornton), 33 (Tomo
Jesenicnik), 34 (Tupungato), 35 (infografick), 38 (Dervin
Witmer), 40 (donatas1205), 41 (Anna Hoychuk), 43 (RoJo
Images), 45 (leolintang), 48 (Josh Resnick), 49 (kuleczka);
Superstock pp.7 (© Ambient Images Inc.), 10 (© Cusp), 18
(© GAP), 32 (© imagebroker.net).

Cover photograph of a girl holding vegetables in a
garden reproduced with permission of Aurora Photos (Big
Cheese Photo). Cover logo reproduced with permission of
Shutterstock (Olivier Le Moal).

Every effort has been made to contact copyright holders
of material reproduced in this book. Any omissions will
be rectified in subsequent printings if notice is given to
the publisher.

All the Internet addresses (URLs) given in this book were
valid at the time of going to press. However, due to the
dynamic nature of the Internet, some addresses may have
changed, or sites may have changed or ceased to exist
since publication. While the author and publisher regret
any inconvenience this may cause readers, no responsibility
for any such changes can be accepted by either the author
or the publisher.

Contents

Some words are shown in bold, **like this**. You can find out what they mean by looking in the glossary.

Important!
Please check with an adult before doing the projects in this book.

Being Green

Being "eco," or environmentally-friendly, is about sparing a thought for the world around you in your daily life. That could mean using less energy or water to reduce pollution and protect natural resources for the future. It could mean doing something to help wildlife or cutting the amount of waste you throw away. With just under 7 billion people on Earth and that number rising, your planet needs your support to stay green and healthy!

However, being eco is not just about doing your part for the planet. It is also about having fun, developing new interests, and making new friends. Eco-gardening is about growing fabulous flowers, fruits, and vegetables in ways that are in tune with nature. Eco-cooking is about using the freshest ingredients in season to create mouthwatering dishes to impress your friends and family.

Making a start

If the projects and advice in this book look a bit intimidating, just try doing one or two things. These will add up to make a big difference. If you like how it is going, then do a few more. That way, green issues won't seem overwhelming. In any case, there are few rules in eco-gardening and cooking. It is more about trying things out and seeing what works for you.

Eco-gardening and cooking are about getting results, like this super-size squash!

Picnics are fun—and even better with foods that contain fresh ingredients that are good for you.

What's in it for me?

- Eco-gardening and cooking are fun, so why not hold a bake-off or cooking contest, offer prizes for the best produce, or organize a tasting session with friends?

- Eco-gardening is a great way to get fresh air and some exercise.

- Growing your own fruits and vegetables can be very satisfying. And what could be more impressive for friends and family than serving up food cooked with your very own ingredients—how cool is that?

- Eco-gardening and cooking are about thinking for yourself and asserting your individuality, which can make you more confident.

- Eco-gardening, shopping, and cooking can save money. You can calculate how much you have saved and then spend that money on an outing, that new top you want, or a new piece of sports equipment.

- Eco-shopping and cooking allow you to take control of what you eat. Home-grown foods and those produced by **organic farming** methods are generally better for you than mass-produced foods and packaged meals containing food additives and other chemicals.

- Eco-gardening and cooking could even help out later in life, as employers are impressed by green credentials and look for people who show a willingness to start projects and try new things.

Green Gardening

Green gardening is incredibly satisfying. A bit of effort will produce great results such as delicious fruits and vegetables or a flower-filled garden alive with bees and butterflies.

Your garden

You don't need a large space to get started. If you have a garden, your parents may let you have a small area. If not, ask your school if you can use a wild corner of the grounds. Join the school gardening club or eco-club—or start one. You could also rent a space with friends or join a community gardening program. Contact your local government to find out what is possible in your area.

To grow strong and healthy, plants need sunlight and protection from severe weather such as wind and frost. Ideally, your gardening area should be on sunny, well-drained soil, with a nearby water source. But many green gardeners work wonders with a less-than-promising plot of land.

This flowchart will help you find a space to garden.

No ← **Is there space to garden at home?** → Yes

Is there space on the school grounds?

Ask if you can use some of it.

No

Yes →

Ask if you can cultivate it. Join or start a gardening club or eco-club.

Is it possible to share a plot or join a community gardening program?

No

Yes →

Join or put your name on the mailing list.

Grow plants in pots, window boxes, or on windowsills indoors.

6

What to grow?

Deciding what to grow is a key decision. It partly depends on the size of your garden and conditions such as soil and climate. You should also think about timing—it won't work to produce a big harvest at a time you are away. Start small, with a few easy-to-grow plants. If you get the gardening bug, expand your horizons. Tips for starters are:

- Tomatoes grow from seed to crop in 14 to 20 weeks.
- Scarlet runner beans grow from seed to crop in 12 to 14 weeks.
- Potatoes produce a crop in 16 to 22 weeks.

Gardening without a garden

If you cannot find an outdoor space, you can still garden in pots, hanging baskets, a window box, or even on windowsills indoors. To grow plants in pots, you will need containers of various sizes. For example, empty yogurt containers are great for seedlings. You can grow zucchini, scarlet runner beans, or tomatoes in an old bucket, and potatoes can grow in a trash can or stack of tires. All the projects in this book can be grown in pots. Peppers, tomatoes, herbs, and sprouting beans can be grown indoors on a sunny windowsill.

Gardening is a matter of trial and error. Don't be afraid to ask other gardeners about what works and what doesn't in your area.

Shallow-rooted plants such as tomatoes, lettuces, and strawberries grow well in pots and hanging containers, but they will need regular watering.

Soil

Soil provides the **nutrients** plants need to grow. That makes it a gardener's most precious resource! Take care of soil, and it will reward you with fantastic flowers, fruits, and vegetables. Soil is made up of **organic matter** (dead plants and animals) plus small pieces of rock. There are five main types of soil, depending on the rock in your area and how it formed: clay, silt, sand, chalk, and peat. Gardeners also talk of loam— a mixed soil that is ideal for gardening. If you have it, you are lucky.

Finding out about soil

Find out what type of soil you have by crumbling a sample in your fingers. Clay is sticky and can be molded into a ball. Silt feels smooth and silky. Sandy soils are coarse and gritty. Chalky soils are gray, dry, and crumbly. Peaty soils are dark. Loam will roll into a crumbly ball.

Here is a way to investigate further: put a soil sample into a jam jar and half-fill the jar with water. Screw the lid on and shake the jar. Leave it for a couple of days. You can then identify the rock that has settled on the bottom.

pH value

Soil can be acidic, neutral, or alkaline. This is called its **pH value**. You can buy a cheap soil-testing kit from a garden center. Many kits register the pH value on a scale numbered 1–14. Acidic soils score under 7, and alkaline soils score 7 and over. Most plants like neutral soil of 6.5–7.

Working with the soil

Each soil type has advantages and disadvantages. Clay does not drain well. It can be heavy and hard to dig, but it is high in nutrients. Silt is quite similar to clay; it has fewer nutrients, but it is easier to dig. Both can get waterlogged in winter and bake dry in summer. Sandy soil drains well, but it can be low in nutrients. Chalky soils are stony and often alkaline. Peat is black and fertile, but it is usually acidic. Loam is easy to work, drains well, and is high in nutrients.

Plants like different types of soil (see the table below). Green gardeners work with nature by growing plants that suit local conditions. For example, grow plants that tolerate wet conditions in clay and silt, and grow ones that cope with dry conditions in sand or chalk. Find out more on pages 50–51. However, don't be discouraged if you discover you do not have the perfect soil for what you want to grow. You can improve soil—for example, by adding compost to sandy and chalky soils. Add lime or wood ash to improve acidic soils such as peat. Follow the instructions on the package when using garden lime.

Acidic soils	Alkaline soils
Flowering plants: Rhododendrons, azaleas, iris, magnolia	Flowering plants: Buddleia, lilac, honeysuckle, clematis, evening primrose
Fruits and vegetables: Potatoes, rhubarb, raspberries, beans, peas, pumpkins	Fruits and vegetables: Broccoli, cabbage, cauliflower, leeks, lettuce, spinach

This table shows some plants that can tolerate acidic and alkaline soils.

Water

No garden can flourish without water. However, many gardeners waste huge amounts. Wasting water depletes local rivers and underground water sources. It is also very expensive if your water is metered. Reducing water use is vital to **eco-friendly** gardening.

Water-saving tips

- Get a "gun" attachment for your hose. This allows you to control flow. Better yet, use a watering can instead of a hose or sprinkler.
- Grow native plants that are suited to local conditions.
- Grow plants that can cope with dry conditions, such as Oriental poppy, sedum, euphorbia, nasturtium, and cistus (rockrose).
- Water in the early morning or evening to reduce moisture lost through evaporation during the day.
- Water the soil at the base of plants, not the plants themselves.
- Cover soil with a **mulch** such as compost or bark chippings to reduce evaporation and weeds (see pages 18–19).
- Save the water you use for washing dishes and cleaning vegetables. This is called "gray water" and can be recycled to water the garden.
- Bear in mind that hanging baskets, window boxes, and pots can dry out quickly and need almost daily watering in the summer.

Make sure you water plants at the base, not on the leaves. Wet leaves can get scorched by direct sunlight, especially during the day.

Eco impact

Watering with a hose or sprinkler uses about half a pint (0.2 liters) of water a second. Using a hose for half an hour can use as much water as a family of four uses in a day.

Build a rain barrel

Harvest the water that falls naturally by installing a rain barrel. You will need to buy a length of drainpipe and connectors to divert water from the gutter. Think carefully about where the rain barrel will be and measure how much pipe you will need. You can find out more on web sites such as www.epa.gov/region3/p2/make-rainbarrel.pdf.

Be safe

- Wear gloves when handling compost, soil, and lime to guard against germs, bacteria, and other hazards. This also prevents your hands from getting dry.
- Wash your hands after you have finished gardening.

Monitoring water use

Investigate the amount of water your family uses in the garden over a two-week period in summer by adapting the measurements below. In week 1, water in the normal way and add up the totals. In week 2, save as much water as possible, and total as before. How much water have you saved?

Activity	Amount used from local water supplies	Mins/times used	Total
hose/sprinkler	3 gallons/min		
hose gun	3 gallons/min		
watering can	1.5 gallons		
rain barrel	0 gallons		
gray water	0 gallons		

Improving soil

Plants use nutrients from the soil as they grow. Adding compost returns those nutrients. You can buy compost from a garden center, but it is much greener and less expensive to make your own. Worms, millipedes, and other creatures called **decomposers** will move in and break down waste to release nutrients. Using kitchen and garden waste to nourish next year's plants has the added bonus of cutting down the huge amount of waste that is polluting the planet.

Build a compost box

You will need:

four posts
planks or pallets to make a box 3 x 3 ft. (1 x 1 m)
hammer and nails

Please ask an adult to supervise this project.

You can make a compost box (see below) or buy a bin. You could even use a garbage can with holes drilled in the bottom.

Method:

1. Lay the planks down to figure out the dimensions of your compost box. Saw planks in half if necessary. Mark the positions of the posts on the ground.

2. Get an adult to help you hammer the posts into the ground. Nail the planks into the posts to form a box. Leave small gaps between them to allow air into the heap.

3. Layer on "green" and "brown" compost (see page 13). Cover with a square of old carpet.

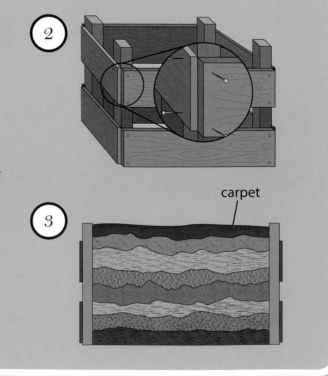

carpet

Feeding compost

Whatever type of compost box or bin you use, follow this method:

- Gradually add equal amounts of "green" and "brown" waste in layers. "Greens" are high in nitrogen and rot quickly. "Browns" are rich in carbon and break down more slowly.
- Put on the bin lid or cover the compost with a square of old carpet to trap heat and encourage decomposers.
- Cover with a plastic sheet in wet weather. Sprinkle the heap with water in dry weather so that it remains moist, but not wet. You do not need to do this if you use a bin with a lid.
- Turn the top layers over with a fork every few months.

Using compost

Decomposers consume organic matter and tunnel through the compost, allowing air inside. In six months, you will have rich, dark compost ready to spread on the garden. Tip the bin upside down or remove compost from near the bottom of the heap. Be careful of animals such as rats that may take shelter in the heap.

Recycling food waste in a compost box or bin can reduce domestic waste by up to one-third.

What to compost

Greens	Browns	Don't use
Fruit & vegetable peelings	Egg cartons	Weeds in seed
Grass cuttings	Cardboard	Cat or dog waste
Soft plant debris	Straw/pet bedding	Cooked food
Cut flowers	Shredded paper	Meat or fish
Nettles and weeds (without seeds)	Shredded wood cuttings	Dairy produce
Used tea bags	Wood shavings	Magazines
		Stale bread

Green gardening made simple

Mastering a few simple techniques such as sowing, **thinning**, and taking cuttings will save money and help your eco-garden to flourish the natural way. For more advice on what to do when throughout the gardening year, see pages 50–51.

Sowing

Growing plants from seed is cheap and greener than buying "ready-made" plants from nurseries that may have been grown using environmentally harmful methods and chemicals.

You will need:

Seeds; an old plastic tray or small yogurt containers with holes drilled to drain water; a mist sprayer; plant labels

Method:

1. Sow seeds indoors in early spring to get a head-start on gardening. Fill the container(s) with peat-free potting compost.

2. Follow the instructions on seed packages when sowing, either scattering seeds or planting them individually. Cover with soil.

3. Water lightly with a mist sprayer. Add popsicle-stick labels to identify seeds. Place on a partly shaded windowsill until the seeds **germinate**.

4. Later in spring, you can transplant the seedlings outdoors, but first, take them outdoors by day and bring them in at night for 10 days, so they can **harden off**.

5. Sow seeds outdoors in late spring, when the weather warms up. Use a stick to make a groove called a **drill** in the soil. Follow the sowing instructions.

Make eco-friendly seed pots

Grow seedlings in newspaper pots that **biodegrade** when planted outside.

Method:

1. Fold a sheet of newspaper in half, then make a second fold about 3 in. (7 cm) from the folded edge.

2. Roll the strip around an empty tin can, so the unfolded ends overlap the open end of the can.

3. Scrunch the overlap inside the can. Remove the can, and use the closed end to crush the pot base flat. Secure with tape if necessary.

4. Fill the pots with potting soil and plant seeds. When the seedlings grow, tear off the base of the pots and place the pots in holes in the soil.

Taking cuttings

You can take cuttings from mature plants to grow new plants. Snip off a side shoot using scissors or pruning shears. Place cuttings that like damp conditions in a glass of water and others in potting compost. Put them in a shady place and mist the leaves regularly. When roots appear, transplant the young plants into their own pots.

Tomatoes

Tomatoes are packed with nutrients and come in different colors, shapes, and sizes. You may like to grow several varieties. If possible, avoid growing standard varieties you can buy in supermarkets. Instead, go for unusual kinds that boost **biodiversity** in the tomato world!

Grow your own tomatoes

You can grow tomato plants bought from a garden center in a grow-bag and nurture them with special tomato fertilizer. But it is far greener to grow them from seed and feed them on a home-grown mix of soil and compost.

Method:

1. Sow tomato seeds in old egg cartons or yogurt containers with holes in the bottom. Fill the containers with soil. Thinly scatter seeds on the surface and cover with about a quarter of an inch (2–3 mm) of soil.

2. Lightly sprinkle with water. Place the containers in a warm, sheltered place to germinate.

3. When seedlings appear, thin them, to allow the strongest to flourish.

4. When true leaves appear, plant seedlings in individual pots. As they grow bigger, re-pot them in pots deep enough to support stakes. Carefully push the stakes into the pots and tie the stems to stakes to support the plants.

5. Pinch or snip off shoots that appear where side stems join main stems. Do this to the growing tip when the plant has about five flowering stems. Moisten the leaves with a water spray.

6. Grow marigolds in the tomato pots to discourage whitefly. If you sow them from seed, start early in the season, or put in young plants. This is called **companion planting**.

7. Tomatoes are ready for picking when they are an even color all over.

Growing basil

Basil is an herb that is great to flavor pizza, soup, or pasta sauce.

Method:

1. Sow basil seeds in pots filled with potting compost in the spring. Put them in a warm place to germinate.

2. When seedlings sprout, you can continue growing them indoors in pots. Or you can harden them off and plant outdoors in a row, leaving 8 inches (20 cm) between plants.

3. Avoid splashing the leaves when you water, because that allows a disease called blight to develop. Harvest leaves from several different plants, to allow each plant time to recover.

Being green: Summing up

- Be a green gardener using a window box, pots, or a corner of your school grounds.
- Mulch and compost return nutrients to the soil.
- Reduce water use in the garden.
- Grow plants that suit local conditions.

Eco-Friendly Gardens

Not all gardening is green! Many gardeners soak their garden with **herbicides** to kill weeds and **pesticides** to control slugs and insects. These poisons enter the food chain to kill other wildlife, such as birds and ladybugs. They can also harm pets, pollute water sources, and leave **toxic** traces in fruits and vegetables. Organic gardeners use fewer chemicals to minimize harm to the environment. **Organic gardening** is kinder to nature—but how do you tackle pests?

Organic gardening tips

- Healthy plants fend off insect invaders more efficiently than sickly ones. So, caring for plants, especially young ones, pays dividends.

- Remove insect pests such as aphids as soon as you spot them. Spraying with soapy water kills aphids, but don't use anti-bacterial soap.

- Cut the bottoms off large plastic drink bottles to create mini-greenhouses, or **cloches**. Place the tops of the bottles over young plants and press them into the soil.

- Drape old net curtains over fruit bushes and plants such as zucchini to deter birds and aphids.

- Drape strings of foil and old CDs over fruit bushes to keep birds away.

A cloche made from a large drink bottle provides a warm, sheltered, bug-free environment for young plants.

Weeds

How can you avoid weeds without spraying toxic weedkiller? One answer is a little regular weeding, either by hand or with a hoe. Get a head start on weeds by tackling them in early spring. Weeding little and often is much easier. You can smother stubborn weeds by putting down an old carpet or mulch such as leaf mold or bark chippings. Weeds are easier to pull up after rain.

However, weeds aren't all bad—caterpillars that grow into butterflies feed on them. Leaving a wild area where weeds are allowed can lure insect pests away from your prize vegetables. Weeds such as dandelions, nettles, and blackberries are edible either raw (blackberries), cooked, or made into tea. Some make tasty treats for pets such as tortoises and rabbits. Clover enriches the soil by adding nitrogen.

Pest control

Predatory bugs such as ladybugs, hoverflies, and lacewings eat aphids, mites, and scale insects. Encourage these helpful insects by planting their favorite food plants, such as coriander, coreopsis, and geraniums.

Ladybugs can eat 50 to 60 aphids a day, as well as other harmful insects such as leafhoppers and mites.

Controlling pests on lettuces

Growing red and green varieties of lettuce adds color and texture to salad, as well as helping biodiversity. But beware—slugs and snails love lettuces. Keeping these pests at bay will test your green gardening skills.

Growing lettuces

1. Grow lettuces from seed in yogurt containers filled with potting compost. Use a pencil to make a series of drills (grooves) in the soil about 12 in. (30 cm) apart.

2. Sow the tiny seeds into the groove as thinly as possible and cover with soil. There should be about three or four seeds every 6 in. (15 cm). Sprinkle or spray with water.

3. When seedlings germinate, thin them to about 6 in. (15 cm) apart, removing small or spindly plants.

4. When seedlings are well grown, transplant them into pots or outdoors. Pick outer leaves of mature lettuces, leaving the plants to produce more leaves.

Sowing batches of lettuce seeds at 10-day intervals will produce a crop that lasts longer.

Green tips

- Start lettuces indoors so they can thrive in a slug-free environment before exposing them to outdoors.
- Slugs and snails are most active at night and in wet weather. These are the times you need to go on slug patrol.
- If all else fails, you can get organic slug killers from garden centers, although these are a less green solution.

Keeping mollusks away

There are three main chemical-free defense strategies against pests: barriers, traps, and predators.

Barriers
- Grow lettuces in a window box or in containers placed on a high shelf or table.
- Mollusks can't move over gritty surfaces, so put down gravel, crushed eggshells, or nutshells.
- Place plastic-bottle cloches over lettuces. This will also help speedy plant growth.

Traps and lures
- Pour milk or beer into plastic pots or tubs. Dig holes and sink the traps into the ground by the lettuce patch. They will attract slugs and put an end to them by drowning—gory but effective.
- Mollusks love the herb comfrey (Symphytum). Lure them away with a pile of fresh-cut comfrey leaves. After a few days, remove the mollusks and compost the comfrey.

Predators
- Frogs, toads, and birds such as thrushes prey on mollusks. You can encourage amphibians by making a mini-pond (see page 25). If you have room, plant a berry bush to attract thrushes.

Gardening for birds

Birds bring any outdoor space to life! They also help green gardeners by controlling pests such as slugs, snails, and caterpillars. Recent years have seen steep declines in songbirds because of **habitat loss**, **climate change**, and the use of chemicals in farming. Help to reverse the trend by making your backyard or window box a bird-friendly zone.

Build a bird table

This bird table will suit any outdoor space

You will need:

an old tray or board about 12 x 8 in. (30 x 20 cm); wooden strips (dowels); hammer; tacks (short nails); 4 eye-hooks; strong wood glue; drill; and strong string or chain

Protect your birds by putting a bell on your cat's collar.

Method:

1. Drill a few holes in the board to drain water.

2. Glue and then tack the wooden strips to the board to form a raised edge, so the bird-food cannot blow off.

3. Fix screws near the corners. Attach two equal lengths of string or chain to the screws. Hang the table from a branch or wall bracket, out of the reach of cats.

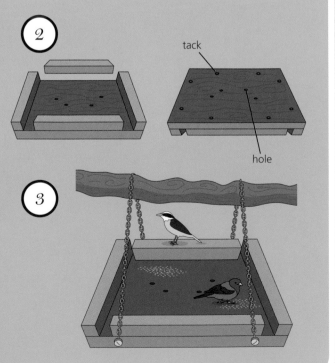

tack

hole

Make bird cake

You will need:

8 oz. (225 g) lard; 1-lb. (500-g) mix of breadcrumbs, nuts, sunflower seeds, oatmeal, and raisins; large yogurt container or half-coconut shell; string

Method:

1. Melt the fat in a pan on a low heat. Pour it into a bowl and add the dry ingredients. Mix well.

2. Make a large knot in a piece of string. Put the knot in the yogurt container. Hold the string upright while you spoon in the mixture.

3. Allow the mixture to cool and set. Then pull the string to remove the cake from the container and hang it outside.

4. Alternatively, hang a half-coconut shell on the string and spoon in the mixture. Allow to set.

Small, acrobatic birds such as titmice are able to balance as they feed from a coconut shell.

Food for birds

Birds enjoy kitchen scraps such as stale cheese, bread, cake, and overripe fruit. Crumble and moisten bread and cake. Overripe apples and oranges can be cut in half and strung up. Keep the area below the table clean, to avoid attracting mice or rats. Be consistent when you commit to feeding birds. They will come to rely on you as a food source. If you need to stop, scale back gradually so that the birds have time to get used to finding other food sources.

Wildlife-friendly garden

You do not need a lot of space to make a mini-reserve for wildlife. A balcony or window box will work. If you do have space, you could make several mini-habitats to suit different creatures such as insects, birds, and frogs. Design your own eco-garden, and then make it a reality in a corner of the school grounds or a patch of waste ground in a city.

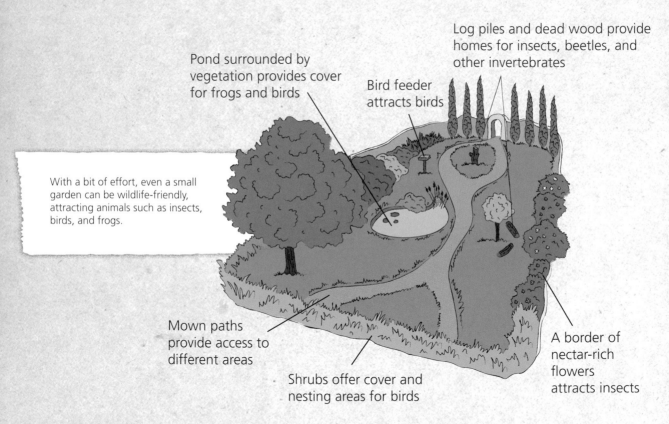

Pond surrounded by vegetation provides cover for frogs and birds

Log piles and dead wood provide homes for insects, beetles, and other invertebrates

Bird feeder attracts birds

With a bit of effort, even a small garden can be wildlife-friendly, attracting animals such as insects, birds, and frogs.

Mown paths provide access to different areas

Shrubs offer cover and nesting areas for birds

A border of nectar-rich flowers attracts insects

Attracting wildlife

- *For bees and butterflies:* Plant verbena, phlox, snapdragons, thyme, marjoram, lavender, and sage.
- *For bees and hummingbirds:* Plant trumpet vine, morning glory, nasturtiums, and delphiniums.
- *For moths and bats:* Plant sweet-smelling honeysuckle, phlox, and evening primrose.

Make a mini-pond

A small pond in a sunny spot will attract frogs, newts, and dragonflies.

You will need:

an old garbage can lid or large bowl; a few rocks and water plants; and bricks

Method:

1. Dig a hole in the ground. Press the container into the hole and fill around the edges with soil.

2. Add rocks or pebbles around the edge. Place rocks in the water near the edge to allow frogs and newts to climb out. Add potted native water plants on bricks.

3. Fill with rainwater from a rain barrel. Add pondweed from a supplier. Top up the pond in dry weather.

Being green: Summing up

- Use organic methods to reduce pests.
- Attract birds to your garden by providing food.
- Create a mini-habitat to attract wildlife.

How Green Is Your Diet?

Growing your own food is a great way to make your diet eco-friendly. However, growing *all* your own food would take too much space, time, and energy. So, what are some other options?

Go organic

The simplest way is to buy organic. Organic and all-natural farmers use similar techniques to green gardeners, such as using manure and compost instead of artificial fertilizers to enrich the soil. Instead of using harmful pesticides, they use companion planting and crop rotation. Field borders are left wild to encourage pest-munching predators such as ladybugs. Organic livestock farmers raise free-range animals on organic crops. Farmers have to meet strict criteria to be certified as organic. Organic food does tend to cost more than food produced by **intensive farming** methods. But many people think it tastes better, and it is guaranteed to contain fewer chemicals.

Organic beef and dairy products come from cattle that are reared on organic feed and often allowed to graze in the open.

Eco impact

Apples sold in supermarkets have been sprayed an average of 35 times. The average supermarket pear has been sprayed 13 times.

These volunteers are working in a community garden—a good way to grow vegetables if you live in a city, where private gardens are rare.

Where can I buy organic?

Organic foods and snacks are now available from a wide range of outlets, such as health food stores, farmers' markets in towns and cities, and farm stores and stalls in the country. Many areas have **community-supported agriculture (CSA)** programs where you can get organic produce delivered to your door. Supermarkets also stock organic foods, but they are more likely to source foods from distant countries, which causes additional pollution.

What to buy?

Realistically, eating only organic foods would probably be too expensive. So, what are the top priorities?

- Some people believe organic fruits and vegetables are healthier than conventionally grown ones that have been sprayed with chemicals. Opt for kinds you do not peel, such as apples, pears, grapes, peaches, spinach, potatoes, tomatoes, and lettuce.
- The cocoa used to make non-organic chocolate is one of the most highly sprayed of all crops, which harms local wildlife and causes illness in the plantation workers who do the spraying.
- Wheat, barley, and rice have a large surface area relative to their mass. This means non-organic varieties have high exposure to chemical sprays.
- Organic cheese, milk, and yogurt come from cows reared in eco-friendly conditions. The same goes for organically produced meat and fish.

Every organic product you buy increases the demand for all-natural foods, which will ultimately help to bring prices down.

Thinking about diet

You may know the saying "You are what you eat." But the food choices we make affect not only ourselves, but also the planet. Most of the world's fertile land is given over to growing food, and with the human population rising rapidly, the impact of farming can only increase.

Vegetarian and vegan

Becoming a vegetarian or **vegan** is the ultimate choice for reducing your "**food footprint**"—the impact your diet has on the planet. While vegetarians have a meat- and fish-free diet, vegans also avoid all animal products such as eggs and dairy. Not eating meat saves land, water, and also reduces **greenhouse gases** that are leading to climate change. Not eating fish helps to preserve ocean wildlife. Not everyone wants to go vegetarian or vegan. But eating a bit less meat and fish as part of a nutritionally balanced diet reduces your impact on the planet.

Eco impact

Studies show that a piece of land that can grow crops to feed 30 people can only produce enough meat, eggs, and milk to feed 5 to 10 people.

Since the 1990s, huge areas of rain forest have been cleared to raise cattle to supply beef to fast-food burger chains and supermarkets.

Opting for some vegetarian meals reduces your **carbon footprint.** When you do eat meat or fish, try to buy food that is sustainably produced.

Eating meat

The greenest meat options are organic and free-range products. Free-range animals are reared in conditions that are less cramped than on conventional farms. Organic livestock are not given **hormones** to increase growth or **antibiotics** to fight infection. These can pollute water supplies, and traces of them end up in non-organic food.

Beef is the most environmentally harmful food of all, using huge amounts of water, land, grain crops, and fish-meal, and causing habitat loss in places such as the Amazon rain forest. Local butchers, farmers' markets, supermarkets, and some restaurants stock free-range meat from nearby farms, or you can buy it online.

Fish

Modern fishing fleets are so good at harvesting fish that not enough fish are left in the oceans to breed. Three-quarters of the world's fisheries are depleted, and many fish species are endangered. Fish farming can help to relieve pressure on wild fish stocks, but it still has an impact on ocean ecosystems, causing habitat loss and pollution.

Buying fish from **sustainable** sources is the best option. Go to www.montereybayaquarium.org/cr/seafoodwatch.aspx to learn more and find recommendations for ocean-friendly seafood. If you buy canned fish such as tuna, opt for "dolphin-safe" brands that catch tuna using nets that allow dolphins to escape.

Be label literate

Reading food labels allows you to investigate your food footprint. Becoming label-savvy also helps you to see through the marketing ploys of supermarkets and food producers—and find out whether foods are genuinely healthy or not.

Food labels show:

- ingredients—listed in order of quantity (largest to smallest)
- country of origin—you can calculate **food miles** (see page 34)
- nutritional information
- additional health information (such as suitability for vegetarians).

Energy—and often water—is used at every stage of food processing. These carrots are being washed in a processing plant before being packaged or further processed.

What's in your food?

The labels on your food may indicate how raw foods, such as chopped nuts, have been processed. Packaged meals, fast foods, and many snacks are highly processed, with produce being cleaned, chopped, cooked, and treated with chemicals. The more highly processed a food is, the greater the eco-impact.

Is it healthy?

Many snacks and cereals are packaged as healthy. Look more closely at the labels, however, and you may spot that the product is also high in salt, fat, or sugar. It may also contain additives, preservatives, and artificial color and flavoring. Reading a few labels on the foods you eat regularly will help you draw some general conclusions and make informed choices about food.

Spot greenwashing

Many foods are now marketed as eco-friendly, with pictures of nature and vague phrases such as "now uses less energy." Such claims should be backed up by concrete information— for example, "packaging made from 50 percent recycled materials"—to have any meaning. Without specific information, these claims are just **greenwashing**—marketing hype aimed at people interested in green issues. Some food manufacturers are working to reduce the eco impact of their products. Others are just pretending to do so. Don't be fooled!

ingredients and nutritional info

additives

eco-claims

country of origin

Packaging problems

Take a look at the contents of your lunch. Does it contain packaged foods and snacks? Food packaging helps protect food and makes it last longer. Eye-catching packaging also persuades us to buy. But the huge amounts of food packaging used create a waste disposal problem.

Food packaging makes up about one-third of all domestic waste in economically developed countries. Most of this ends up in **landfills**, where it may pollute soil and water. Otherwise, it is burned, creating toxic ash and air pollution. The manufacture of packaging also consumes natural resources and energy and causes pollution.

Recycling glass saves minerals and energy.

Metal cans are cheap and easy to recycle.

Recycling paper and cardboard saves timber and reduces water pollution.

Plastic lasts hundreds of years. Many kinds cannot be recycled.

Cut down on packaging

Reduce the eco-impact of food packaging by following the three Rs of waste disposal—Reduce, Reuse, and Recycle.

Reduce waste

- Choose products with less packaging.
- Buy loose fruits and vegetables whenever you can.
- Buy one or two large items instead of several small ones.

Reuse

- Buy refillable containers and refills rather than new products. Return refillable bottles.
- Use cloth bags or reuse plastic bags.
- Reuse plastic tubs and containers, glass jars, and egg cartons to plant seedlings or hold pens and pencils.

Recycle

- Recycle packaging that you cannot reuse at recycling centers or through curbside pickup programs.
- Buy items made from recycled materials.
- Choose glass, metal, and cardboard packaging over plastic, as they are easier to recycle.

Eco impact

The cost of packaging represents up to 16 percent of the cost of each food item you buy.

Can you make a change?

Calculate how much of the food packaging you use can be reduced:

1. Sort food packaging at home by materials. Bag glass, metal, paper/cardboard, plastic, and food waste separately. Weigh the bags. Compare their size and estimate their volume. Do this for a week.
2. In the second week, reduce as much waste as possible by following the three Rs. Separate and weigh the materials as before. Which material have you been most effective in reducing by weight, and which by volume?

Food miles

What is your favorite fruit? Is it grown locally or in another part of the world? One of the easiest ways to make your diet greener is to choose foods grown locally, because this reduces food miles, the distance foods must travel to reach you.

Supermarkets stock a huge range of produce, much of it flown or shipped from farms thousands of miles away. Food miles are a major source of greenhouse gases. Transporting food uses up huge amounts of **fossil fuels**, which are now becoming scarce. It also uses up other resources such as packaging, because foods that are traveling long distances require protection. Think about your favorite meal. Are the ingredients sourced locally or abroad? Find out more about the food miles involved in particular foods by visiting www. organiclinker.com/ food-miles.cfm.

Produce sold at farmers' markets is likely to have traveled relatively short distances from field to stall.

Eco impact

Recent studies show that fresh produce travels over 1,500 miles (2,400 kilometers) on average from food to table in the United States, and processed foods travel over 1,300 miles (2,100 kilometers).

Buy local produce

Fruits and vegetables grown locally are likely to have a lower **carbon impact** than, say, mangoes grown thousands of miles away, because they have traveled a shorter distance. So, where can you buy local produce? The list of outlets is pretty much the same as for organic foods: farm stores, farmers' markets, CSA programs, and local and health food stores. You can also order them online. Buying direct from farmers helps to reduce food waste, since supermarkets reject a lot of produce that is fine to eat but looks less than perfect. Another way is to grow your own food—you cannot get more local than that! Supermarkets may also stock some locally grown foods alongside similar produce transported huge distances.

Most beef used in U.S. burgers comes from Brazil, where cattle ranching causes habitat destruction. Cereals and seeds for buns may have traveled long distances. Lettuce and the ingredients used in mayonnaise may also have a high eco impact.

Green tips

- Check food labels for the country of origin. Choose locally grown foods over ones involving high food miles.
- When you do buy exotic foods with high food miles, look for **Fair Trade** labels. Fair trade goods such as chocolate and bananas offer farmers in developing countries a reasonable price for their crops.
- Car journeys to and from supermarkets use fuel and produce greenhouse gases, adding to the amount of carbon dioxide in the atmosphere. Sometimes you can reduce this pollution by ordering online and requesting home delivery. One van making many deliveries is more **energy-efficient** than individual car journeys.

Eco-Cooking and the Green Kitchen

Eco-cooking and a green kitchen will help save resources such as energy, food, and water. It will also save you money! Use fresh ingredients to whip up dishes to impress your friends and family.

Energy in the kitchen

Kitchens use more energy than any other room in the house. They are packed with appliances such as refrigerators, microwaves, and stoves. Some of these items are essential; others save work, but they gobble up energy, increasing carbon footprints and causing pollution.

Look around your kitchen. How many items use up energy? Can you avoid using some of them?

Green kitchen

Trying just some of these tips will make a difference:

- Don't put warm foods in the refrigerator. Wait until they are completely cold.
- Don't leave the refrigerator or freezer door open. For each minute open, it will take 3 to 4 minutes for the appliance to regain temperature.
- Defrosting frozen foods overnight reduces the energy used in refrigeration.
- Microwaves are more energy-efficient than ordinary stoves, especially when defrosting and warming up food and cooking foods such as baked potatoes.
- When cooking on a stove top, put lids on pans when possible, and cut food into small pieces to reduce cooking time. Don't use a larger pan than you need.
- Maximize oven use by cooking several dishes at once.
- Don't open the oven door more than you have to.

For tips on saving water, see pages 46–47.

More energy-saving tips

- Leaving machines on standby wastes energy. Switch them off if possible.
- Use energy-saving lightbulbs in the kitchen and elsewhere.
- Ask your family to consider switching to a green energy supplier. Still better, could you fit solar panels to the roof?

Reducing energy in the kitchen

Energy is measured in **kilowatt hours**. Use an energy monitor or take energy readings to find out how much energy you use in the kitchen. You may be able to get a free energy monitor by searching online. Measure the energy used by each appliance for a minute and multiply by the number of minutes used. Measure refrigerator and freezer energy use by switching off all other machines. Fill in the values as shown and total over a weekend. Over a second weekend, make all the energy savings you can and recalculate energy use. How much energy have you saved? You could also use the price per unit shown on your energy bill to figure out how much money you have saved.

activity	kw/min (1 unit)	total units used	weekend total
boiling kettle			
refrigerator			
freezer			
microwave			
oven			
dishwasher			
toaster			

Harvest time

Growing your own fruits and vegetables is a great way to make sure you have the freshest, healthiest ingredients to cook with. However, in bumper years (years with good harvests) you can end up with a **glut** (surplus) of certain crops. How can you avoid waste, make the most of the harvest, and make it last through the year?

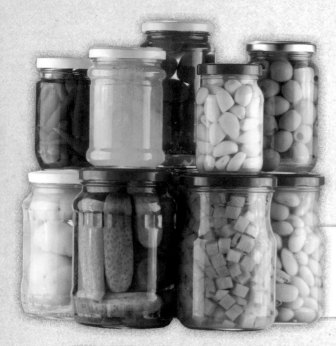

Storing, freezing, canning, and drying foods makes them last six months or more. You can also turn surplus fruits and vegetables into sauces, pickles, and jams. Swap fresh produce with friends, relatives, or within your eco-club. Or invite your friends to a seasonal feast of fresh-picked produce!

Even if you don't grow your own, you can still buy cheap fruits and vegetables in season and preserve them. You can also gather wild foods in season.

Preserving the harvest

- Storing: Fruits and vegetables last longer stored in cloth bags in a cool, dry place. Potatoes are best stored in the dark. String and hang onions and garlic to allow air to circulate. Apples are best packed in paper in a box.
- Freezing: Soft fruits, beans, and other produce keep for up to six months frozen. Wash, dry, and pack them in plastic containers.
- Drying: Dried tomatoes, peppers, chilis, and apricots burst with flavor. Dry produce on a tray in a greenhouse, conservatory, or on a sunny windowsill for three to four days until leathery.
- Canning: You will need some glass jars with lids and airtight seals. Sterilize the jars in boiling water. Pack the fruit into the jar to within just under 1 inch (2 cm) of the top. Fill to the brim with water. Screw the lid on tightly, and stand it in a saucepan of boiling water for 20 minutes. Water should cover the whole jar. When cold, label the jars so you know what is in them and when they were made, and store them in a cool, dark place.

Harvest berry smoothie

Serves 1

You will need:

2 handfuls of any soft fruit in season, such as strawberries,
    raspberries, blackberries, or blueberries
1 tsp honey
5 fl. oz. (150 ml) natural yogurt

Method:

1. Put the ingredients in a blender or a tall glass if using a handheld blender.

2. Blend until smooth and creamy. Add more fruit to taste.

Quick tomato sauce

You will need:

5½ lbs. (2.5 kg) ripe tomatoes
1 finely chopped onion, 1 clove garlic, crushed
3½ fl. oz. (100 ml) olive oil or large piece of butter
2 tsp mixed herbs; 2 bay leaves; pinch of paprika
salt and pepper to taste

Method:

1. Put all ingredients except tomatoes in a pan and
   cook on low heat for 10 minutes. Stir regularly.

2. Add the tomatoes and cook for 30 minutes
   (12–15 minutes in microwave) to make a thick
   mixture. Stir from time to time.

3. Freeze when cold and then defrost to make an
   instant sauce for pasta.

Green cooking

What we cook and how we cook it both have an impact on the planet. Eco-cooking is about reducing your food footprint. The issues take a bit of thinking through, but if everyone does even a few practical things, it adds up to a lot.

Make an eco-chili

To make an eco-friendly dish such as a chili, first think about the ingredients. To make it truly eco, you could leave out the meat and add more beans and vegetables. If you feel meat adds a special something you cannot do without, try to buy locally reared, organic beef.

You can reduce food miles by buying local dairy produce and local vegetables in season. Improvise by adding seasonal vegetables such as carrots, celery, and corn. Use your own if possible! Buying local tomatoes in season will reduce food miles, but remember that fruit grown locally in specially heated tunnels could have as high a carbon footprint as fruit shipped from abroad.

Now for the cooking! Microwaves are more energy-efficient than ordinary ovens, but they destroy some of the nutrients in food. A tight-fitting lid on a saucepan or frying pan will save energy. If you use a saucepan, you could steam vegetables in a steamer placed on the pan, to make a side dish. Another eco-option would be to make enough for two meals and freeze half.

Green tips

A home-grown or locally grown salad makes the perfect side dish for a chili. Use whatever is in season with a drizzle of dressing.

Eco-chili

Serves 4, preparation and cooking time: 1 hour

You will need:

2 tablespoons oil
1 large onion, chopped
1–3 teaspoons chili powder or 1 fresh chili, seeded and chopped
1 clove garlic, crushed or chopped fine
1 red pepper, seeded and chopped
4 tablespoons tomato puree
16-oz. (400-g) can of chopped tomatoes or fresh tomatoes, chopped
16-oz. (400-g) can of kidney beans, drained
20 oz. (500 g) lean ground beef. Alternatively use vegetables, such as finely sliced carrots and/or celery
For the topping: 6 oz. (150 g) grated cheddar cheese
1 small carton sour cream

Method:

1. Fry the onions and garlic in a large frying pan or saucepan over low heat until soft, stirring constantly.

2. Add the chili and then the beef and/or sliced vegetables, except the pepper. Stir until the meat is brown or the vegetables are soft.

3. Add the beans, tomato puree, and tomatoes. Add water if the mix seems dry.

4. Bring to a boil, reduce heat, and simmer for 20–30 minutes, adding water if necessary. Stir occasionally.

5. Add red pepper 5–10 minutes before you finish cooking.

6. Serve in bowls. Add a topping of grated cheese and/or sour cream. Serve with rice, tortilla chips, or tacos.

Serve local cheese bought from a farmers' market.

Use homemade tomato sauce (see page 41) instead of tomato puree.

Use locally reared organic beef from a butcher or try the veggie option!

Food waste

Did you know that up to one-third of all the food we buy gets wasted? A lot of this is bargain offers bought on impulse, which then sit in the refrigerator or pantry until we throw them out. Waste food sent to landfills breaks down to release methane, a very powerful greenhouse gas that is worse than carbon dioxide (CO_2). Wasting food is also a huge waste of money!

The three Rs

Follow the three Rs to cut food waste:

Reduce

- Beware of bargain offers such as "2 for 1." It's not cheap if it gets thrown away!
- Make a shopping list and stick to it. Check the contents of the pantry and the refrigerator before you shop, so you only buy what you need.
- Buy fruits and vegetables loose.
- Don't go shopping when you are hungry, as you are more likely to buy snacks!
- Check the refrigerator and pantry regularly for foods that are nearing their "Best before" date. If it's past, it doesn't necessarily mean the food should be thrown out. Use your common sense, and see www.fsis.usda.gov/Factsheets/Food_Product_dating/.

Reuse

- Leftovers such as bread, cooked rice, and potatoes can be made into delicious dishes (see page 45).

Recycle

- Fruit and vegetable peelings, old salad, eggshells, and coffee grounds can go on the compost heap. Some scraps can be used to feed birds (see page 23).

Eco impact

U.S. studies show that 14 to 15 percent of household food is wasted, totaling $43 billion in 2004. One study estimated that halving food waste in the United States would reduce harmful environmental impacts by a quarter, reducing the use of fertilizers, pesticides, and landfills.

Leftovers

Leftovers can be transformed into delicious meals and snacks.

- Cooked potatoes can be made into potato salad, potato cakes, mashed potatoes, and more.
- Cooked rice can be used to make fried rice, soup, or rice pudding.
- Stale bread can be transformed into French toast or bread pudding.
- Leftover roast meat can be used in stews, casseroles, or sandwiches.
- Remains of stews and casseroles can be recycled to make soup.

Bread pudding

You will need:

1 lb., 4 oz. (500 g) bread
1 lb., 4 oz. (500 g) mixed dried fruit
1¼ tbsp mixed spice
20 fl. oz. (600 ml) milk
2 large eggs, beaten
¾ cup (140 g) sugar
7 tbsp (100 g) butter, melted

Method:

1. Tear up the bread and mix with the fruit and spice in a bowl.

2. Add the eggs, milk, sugar, and melted butter and mix well.

3. Tip the mixture into a greased baking sheet and bake in the oven at 350°F for 1.5 hours, until golden.

4. Cut into squares and serve warm with cream, custard, or ice cream, or cold as a snack.

Water in the kitchen

Kitchens clearly use more water than any other room in the house, except the bathroom. Excessive water use can overstretch local water sources such as rivers and underground aquifers. All the water that drains away must be purified before it is recycled, which uses energy. Reducing water use in the kitchen is essential to being eco-friendly.

Tips for saving water

- Don't overfill saucepans and kettles.
- Get leaking faucets fixed as soon as possible.
- Wash fruits and vegetables in a bowl of water, not under the faucet. You can recycle this water on your garden afterward.
- Steam vegetables in a steamer over a saucepan of food.
- Washing dishes by hand usually uses less water than a dishwasher. Rinse soapy dishes in a bowl of clean water. This water can also be used in the garden.
- If you use a dishwasher, wait until you have a full load before you start the wash cycle.

Eco impact

A dripping faucet wastes at least 0.2 gallons (1 liter) of water an hour. If the drips form a stream, you could waste 0.2 gallons (1 liter) every five minutes!

In the United States, an average family of four uses over 100 gallons (400 liters) of water in the kitchen every day!

Calculating water use in the kitchen

Investigate water use in your kitchen using the measurements given below. Make a chart as shown and get family members to tick a column each time they use water. Total the amounts at the end of a weekend. Over a second weekend, put water saving into practice, tick the columns, and total as before. How much water have you saved?

ideas for saving water	water used	weekend 1: times used	weekend 1 totals
fill kettle	0.4 gallons	LHT III	
wash fruits & vegetables under faucet	2.5–4 gallons	IIII	
rinse dishes under the faucet	5.5–8 gallons	III	
dishwasher	13–16 gallons	III	

ideas for saving water	water used	weekend 2: times used	weekend 2 totals
less water in kettle	0.1–0.3 gallon	LHT II	
wash fruit & vegetables in a bowl	1 gallon	IIII	
rinse dishes in a bowl	2 gallons	IIII	
dishwasher (full load only)	13–16 gallons	II	

Detergent pollution

Did you know traces of detergent, surface cleaner, and toxic bleach from kitchens end up in local rivers and streams, where they can harm fish and other wildlife? Use just enough detergent to make a froth, but not so much that there are lots of bubbles. Or buy eco-friendly products. Avoid using bleach altogether. You can even make your own cleaner using a half-and-half mix of water and vinegar, with a squeeze of lemon juice.

Eco-cooking made easy

Buying organic, food miles, avoiding food waste, reducing packaging, energy, water … there's a lot to think about in the green kitchen! But stay cool, because eco-cooking is not about following strict rules. It's about using your creativity to adapt recipes to suit your needs. Green cooking does not need to be complicated. There is nothing more satisfying than creating a fantastic meal from the freshest, crunchiest ingredients—or maybe just from whatever is in the refrigerator.

Steam- or stir-fry feast

A steam-fry is a stir-fry with a lid on, to seal in the flavor!

You will need:

1 tbsp oil, plus seasoning such as garlic, ginger (fresh if possible), onion or scallion, fresh coriander, 1 tbsp soy sauce, lime, or lemon juice
Tofu, shrimp, thinly sliced chicken, pork, or beef, or top with roasted cashews
Use vegetables in season

Method:

1. Chop the vegetables.

2. Add the spices and seasoning to the oil in a medium-hot wok or large frying pan and cook for about 2 minutes, stirring constantly. In a wok, the food should sizzle steadily, but not violently.

3. Add the other ingredients with a little water and cook for 5 to 10 minutes, with the lid on, stirring regularly. Serve with noodles or rice.

Make an eco-friendly meal

Plan an eco-meal using some of the tips in this book. For starters, you could serve soup made from freshly picked vegetables, or maybe sliced vegetables and dips. A stir-fry or steam-fry is quick and easy. For dessert, you could whip up a fruit compote by simmering chopped fruit and a little water in a pan for five minutes. Serve with yogurt, cream, or ice cream.

Fruit crumble

You will need:

Any fruit in season
For the crumble:
1¼ cup (150 g) flour
7 tbsp (100 g) butter or margarine, cut
   into small pieces
⅓ cup (75 g) sugar

Method:

1. Mix the crumble in a bowl.

2. Chop the fruit, place in a dish, and spoon the crumble on top.

3. Bake in a 400°F oven for 35 minutes.

4. Serve with custard, cream, or ice cream.

Being green: Summing up
- Reduce energy and water use in the kitchen.
- Can, freeze, and dry foods in season.
- Reduce food waste.

More Hints and Tips

The gardening year

Spring (March, April, May): Put up birdhouses, sow seeds indoors, prune shrubs, dead-head flowers. Then, later, sow seeds outdoors, plant hanging baskets, get ahead with weeding, add compost to the garden, check for pests, and protect young plants from late frosts.

Summer (June, July, August): Weed garden, thin seedlings, sow seeds in succession (see the bottom box on page 51), watch for pests, dead-head flowers, add mulch to soil, begin major harvest, water as needed, sow seeds for the fall.

Fall (September, October, November): Continue to harvest and store produce, plant bulbs, dig over soil, dead-head flowers, plant shrubs, protect plants from frost, save and label seeds, weed.

Winter (December, January, February): Check stored produce, clean and store garden tools, dig over soil, add compost and mulch, sow early seeds indoors, check frost protection of plants.

Produce by season

spring	summer	fall	winter
asparagus, broccoli, kale, lettuce, rhubarb, spinach, spring greens	asparagus, beans, carrots, cherries, corn, cucumber, currants, eggplant, garlic, lettuce, onions, peas, potatoes, radishes, spinach, strawberries, summer cabbage, tomatoes, turnips, zucchini	apples, blackberries, Brussel sprouts, cabbage, carrots, celery, leeks, onions, peaches, pears, plums, radishes, raspberries, spinach, potatoes, pumpkin, squash, turnips	Brussel sprouts, cauliflower, leeks, lettuce, parsnips, spinach, turnips, winter radish

Plants that grow well in certain soils

Plants for clay soil: Delphiniums, sunflowers, cornflowers, day lilies, asters

Plants for silty soil: Roses, honeysuckle, primrose, witch hazel

Plants for chalky soil: Lilac, buddleia, anemones, primrose, honeysuckle, clematis

Plants for sandy soil: Pampas grass, artemisia, oregano

Plants for peaty soil: Magnolia, witch hazel

Save energy-serve it raw!

Find recipes for these suggestions on the Internet or in cookbooks:

Starters

Sliced peppers, carrots, celery, served with dips

Guacamole is a delicious and easy avocado starter

Gazpacho is a cold tomato-based soup, usually served in summer

Melon with garnish

Main courses

Serve a rainbow salad on the side or as the main feature

Sushi—stylish Japanese dishes made with some raw ingredients

Desserts and drinks

Fresh seasonal fruit salad served with cream or ice cream

Fruit smoothies

Green tips

Sow batches of seeds from a package at 10-day intervals. You will get a crop that lasts longer, instead of all coming at once. This is called **sowing in succession**.

Glossary

antibiotics medicines used to fight infection caused by bacteria in humans or animals

biodegrade break down naturally

biodiversity variety of plants and animals in a particular habitat or the world

carbon footprint measure of the impact you have on the planet, related to the amount of greenhouse gases produced in your daily life through burning fossil fuels for energy

carbon impact *see* carbon footprint

climate change rising temperatures worldwide, caused by the increase of greenhouse gases in the atmosphere that trap the Sun's heat

cloche glass or plastic cover placed over a plant to act as a mini-greenhouse

community-supported agriculture (CSA) practice in which a group of people work together to support local farms. Members pay agreed-upon fees, and in return they receive supplies of food—including fruits and vegetables, but also sometimes things like meat and dairy—as it is available.

companion planting practice of growing two crops or plants together—for example, to discourage pests. In farming, this is known as intercropping.

crop rotation practice of changing the crops that are grown in fields or garden plots from year to year. This prevents the soil from being drained of nutrients.

decomposer living thing that breaks down organic matter

drill groove in which seeds are sown

eco-friendly action that sustains the environment

energy-efficient using as little energy as possible for a task

fair trade movement to ensure that farmers in developing countries get a fair price for their produce

food footprint impact of your diet on the planet

food miles distance that foods travels from the point of origin to your table

fossil fuel fuel such as coal or oil, which was formed over millions of years from the remains of animals or plants

germinate cause to sprout or grow

glut surplus—for example, of a crop

greenhouse gas one of a group of gases, including carbon dioxide and methane, that contribute to global warming

greenwashing making a misleading claim about the environmental benefits of a product or service

habitat loss when a natural habitat is destroyed or altered by people

harden off when young plants are prepared for being planted outdoors by being exposed to daytime temperatures

herbicide poison used to kill weeds

hormone chemical that regulates the working of cells or controls a function, such as growth

intensive farming type of agriculture in which farmers use chemicals and modern machinery and methods to produce a high yield per acre

kilowatt hour measurement of electricity use over an hour. A kilowatt hour is when you use 1,000 watts of energy in an hour—for example, using a 1,000-watt oven for one hour.

landfill area of land where large amounts of waste material are buried under the earth

mulch organic matter, such as leaves, straw, bark chippings, or peat, that is placed around the base of plants to improve the quality of the soil

nutrient chemical that nourishes living things

organic farming method of farming that minimizes the use of harmful chemical fertilizers and pesticides. Organic farming is also known as all-natural farming.

organic gardening method of gardening that minimizes the use of harmful chemical fertilizers and pesticides—for example, to kill pests

organic matter dead plants and animals

pesticide chemical used to kill insects or other organisms that are harmful to crops

pH value whether soil or a solution is chemically neutral, acid, or alkaline

sowing in succession when seeds are sown at time intervals so the harvest occurs over a longer time

sustainable way of doing something that does not use up too many natural resources or pollute the environment

thinning when gardeners weed out seedlings to allow the remaining seedlings to flourish

toxic poisonous

vegan person who does not eat meat, fish, or animal products such as eggs and dairy

Find Out More

Further reading

Gay, Kathlyn. *Living Green: The Ultimate Teen Guide*. Lanham, Md.: Scarecrow, 2012.

Green, Jen. *Food and Farming* (Impact of Environmentalism).Chicago: Heinemann Library, 2012.

Hamilton, Geoff. *Organic Gardening*. New York: Dorling Kindersley, 2011.

Sivertsen, Linda, and Tosh Sivertsen. *Generation Green: The Ultimate Teen Guide to Living an Eco-Friendly Life*. New York: Simon Pulse, 2008.

Stern, Sam, and Susan Stern. *Cooking Up a Storm: The Teen Survival Cookbook*. Cambridge, Mass.: Candlewick, 2006.

Web sites

www.audubon.org
FInd out about efforts to protect birds.

www.epa.gov/osw/conserve/materials/organics/food/fd-house.htm
This Environmental Protection Agency (EPA) page has tips for reducing household food waste.

www.epa.gov/watersense
This EPA page provides tips on saving water.

www.fao.org
The Food and Agriculture Organization of the United Nations will keep you up-to-date with news about food production worldwide.

www.garden.org
Learn more about gardening at this web site.

www.montereybayaquarium.org/cr/seafoodwatch.aspx
This site has information about ocean-friendly seafood choices.

wwf.panda.org/what_we_do/footprint/agriculture
Learn about sustainable farming on WWF's web site.

www.sustainabletable.org
Sustainable Table is a group that supports and encourages sustainable food, farming, and land use.

www.vrg.org/teen
The Vegetarian Resource Group's web site has a section for young people that answers all sorts of questions about vegetarianism.

DVDs

Food, Inc, director Robert Kenner (Magnolia, 2009)

An Inconvenient Truth, director Davis Guggenheim (Paramount, 2006)

More topics to research

Once you have read this book, you might like to research more about eco-gardening and cooking. Try the following subjects to start with:

- organic gardening
- vegetarianism
- reducing food waste
- food miles
- GM foods.

Answers to quiz (page 36):
A: summer; B: winter; C: spring; D: fall

Index